In Your Sixties and Still Crazy!

THIS IS A PRION BOOK

First published in Great Britain in 2016 by Prion
An imprint of the Carlton Publishing Group
20 Mortimer Street
London W1T 3JW

A CIP catalogue for this book is available from the British Library.

ISBN 978-1-85375-957-4

Printed in Dubai

10 9 8 7 6 5 4 3

In Your
Sixties
and Still Crazy!

Humorous and Inspirational Quotes
for those Aged 60 and Beyond

PRION

Contents

Introduction

Sixty? Is it the new 40 or the dawning of a new era of life? Perhaps you're ready to ignore the aches and pains, and embrace a new decade of fun and adventure. On the other hand, you may be happier with a comfortable chair and a lively mind.

The writers, personalities and historical figures whose words are collected here all have different takes on the ageing process. Some of their observations are humorous, some profound, but whether you're just approaching 60 or well into your seventh decade, you'll definitely find plenty of wit and wisdom to interest, stimulate and entertain you.

The Upside
of Being in
Your Sixties

"Birthdays are good for you.
Statistics show that the people who
have the most live the longest."

Larry Lorenzoni

"Eventually you will reach a point
when you stop lying about your age
and start bragging about it."

Will Rogers

"Getting old has its advantages.
I can no longer read the
bathroom scales."

Brad Schreiber

"With age, I am able to appreciate
the beauty in small things more
than when I was younger, perhaps
because I pay attention more."

Jane Fonda

"Ageing is not lost youth, but a new
stage of opportunity and strength."

Betty Friedan

"As a man grows older he either
talks more and says less or talks less
and says more."

Anon

"You can't be as old as I am without waking up with a surprised look on your face every morning. 'Holy Christ, what do you know – I'm still around!' It's absolutely amazing that I survived all the booze and smoking and the cars and the career."

Paul Newman

"Whenever I get down about life going by too quickly, what helps me is a little mantra that I repeat to myself: at least I'm not a fruit fly."

Ray Romano

"I look forward to being older, when what you look like becomes less and less an issue, and what you are is the point."

Susan Sarandon

"As human beings we value the experience that comes with age. We are reminded over and over again with statements like 'older and wiser' and 'respect your elders,' promoting age as something to be cherished and respected."

Jenna Morasca

"I think so much of what we learn when we get older is being comfortable in our own skin and learning what looks good, and not being so trend-centric."

Meghan Markle

"Old age may have its limitations and challenges, but in spite of them, our latter years can be some of the most rewarding and fulfilling of our lives."

Billy Graham

"Thanks to a fabulous armoury of anti-ageing weapons, including exercise, Botox, highlights and increasingly creative corsetry, 60 doesn't look like 60 anymore."

Emma Soames

"As we get older, because of all that we have experienced and surmounted during our lives, many women over 60 find themselves feeling more optimistic about life than ever before."

Margaret Manning

"As you grow old, you lose interest in sex, your friends drift away and your children often ignore you. There are other advantages, of courses but these are the outstanding ones."

Richard Needham

"As I have gotten older, I've discovered the joys of being lazy."

Julie Bowen

"I just want to keep at it. I can't wait to see, after years of being around, the roles I can play when I'm a crazy old lady."

Tanya Fischer

"I'm really in retirement. My career is over. I'm just playing now and having a great time. I like to keep busy and I'm doing what's fun for me."

Dick Van Dyke

"One of the stereotypes I see breaking is the idea of ageing and older women not being beautiful."

Annie Leibovitz

"I'm very comfortable in my own skin now. I started just being myself more and more. For women, this happens as you get older."

Gloria Estefan

"Old age: the crown of life, our play's last act."

Cicero

"The whiter my hair becomes,
the more ready people are to
believe what I say."

Bertrand Russell

"I mourn the young girl, but I think
that what replaces that is a kind of
a liberation, sort of letting go
of having to hold on to that."

Michelle Pfeiffer

"Just remember, once you're over
the hill you begin to pick up speed."

Charles Schulz

"Inside some of us is a thin person struggling to get out, but she can usually be sedated by a few pieces of chocolate cake."

Jo Brand

"When grace is joined with wrinkles, it is adorable. There is an unspeakable dawn in happy old age."

Victor Hugo

"Some day you will be old enough to start reading fairy tales again."

C. S. Lewis

"Old age has its pleasures, which, though different, are not less than the pleasures of youth."

W. Somerset Maugham

"As any Brit will understand, things get a little easier when you don't have to be number one any more. Really, the fall of an empire is not as bad as everyone thinks. It's like retirement. People fear retirement, but it can turn out to be rather pleasant."

John Oliver

"Old age, believe me, is a good and pleasant thing. It is true you are gently shouldered off the stage, but then you are given such a comfortable front stall as spectator."

Confusius

"One of the best parts of growing older? You can flirt all you like since you've become harmless."

Liz Smith

"One of the good things about getting older is you find you're more interesting than most of the people you meet."

Lee Marvin

"Our wrinkles are our medals of the passage of life. They are what we have been through and who we want to be."

Lauren Hutton

"Slow down and enjoy life. It's not only the scenery you miss by going too fast — you also miss the sense of where you are going and why."

Eddie Cantor

"That number doesn't mean a thing. It just doesn't."

Tina Turner

"One of the many pleasures of old age is giving things up."

Malcolm Muggeridge

"The elderly don't drive that badly;
they're just the only ones with time
to do the speed limit."

Jason Love

"The older the fiddler,
the sweeter the tune."

Irish proverb

"They tell you that you'll lose your
mind when you grow older. What
they don't tell you is that you won't
miss it very much."

Malcolm Cowley

"This is the good news. Of memory, hearing, all the faculties, the last to leave us is sexual desire and the ability to make love. That means long after we're wearing bi-focals or hearing aids, we'll be making love. But we won't know with whom or why."

Jack Paar

"You aren't really 60. Just 21 with 39 years experience!"

Anon

"When you reach a certain age, you realise that life is finite. You can be depressed by that or you can say, 'I'm going to appreciate every minute to its maximum potential.'"

Sting

"Whether 60 or 16, there is in every human being's heart the lure of wonder, the unfailing childlike appetite of what's next and the joy of the game of living."

Samuel Ullman

The Downside of Being in Your Sixties

"There was a time when I was into acid and finding the most hip joint in town. Now I'm into antacid and hip joints."

Garrison Keillor

"I guess I don't so much mind being old, as I mind being fat and old."

Benjamin Franklin

"Every man wants to live long, but no man wants to be old."

Jonathan Swift

"At 20 you have the face God has given you… At 40 you have the face life has given you… At 60 you have the face you deserve."

Anon

"After a man passes 60, his mischief is mainly in his head."

Washington Irving

"You know you're 60 when your back goes out more than you do."

Anon

"First you forget names, then you forget faces, then you forget to pull your zipper up, then you forget to pull your zipper down."

Leo Rosenberg

"I used to be able to party all weekend. Now one night of drinking requires more recovery time than minor surgery."

Anon

"I need to retire from retirement."

Sandra Day O'Connor

"Age does take it out of you, and
I haven't the energy I had before.
Sometimes I have breakfast and sit
in this chair, and I wake up and it is
lunchtime. In the past, the idea of
sleeping through a morning would
have horrified me, but you have to
accept the limitations that old age
imposes on you."

Tony Benn

"By the time you're 80 you've
learned everything. Too bad you
can't remember any of it."

George Burns

"Did you ever stop to think and forget to start again?"

Steven Wright

"Nothing makes me feel so old as having to scroll down to find my year of birth..."

Anon

"How little remains of the man I once was, save the memory of him! But remembering is only a new form of suffering."

Charles Baudelaire

"I always have trouble
remembering three things: faces,
names and – I can't remember
what the third thing is."

Fred Allen

"As a young man I used to have four
supple members and one stiff one.
Now I have four stiff and one supple."

Henri Duc d'Aumale

"I think that retirement is the first
step towards the grave."

Hugh Hefner

"Old age is like a plane flying through a storm. Once you are aboard there is nothing you can do about it."

Golda Meir

"I remember things that happened 60 years ago, but if you ask me where I left my car keys five minutes ago, that's sometimes a problem."

Lou Thesz

"Old age: I fall asleep during the funerals of my friends."

Mason Cooley

"At 60, your hair becomes a cosmic joke. It moves from your head to your ears and your nose. And you can't see it without one of those giant funhouse mirrors."

Greg Tamblyn

"Why am I getting older and wider instead of older and wiser?"

Anon

"Old age comes on suddenly and not gradually, as is thought."

Emily Dickinson

"I think the problems with being older come when your body cannot do what your mind wants. Then, Houston, we have a problem."

Antonio Banderas

"It is utterly false and cruelly arbitrary to put all the play and learning into childhood, all the work into middle age, and all the regrets into old age."

Margaret Mead

"Most women have learned a great deal about how to set goals for our First Adulthood and how to roll with the punches when we hit a rough passage. But we're less prepared for our Second Adulthood as we approach life after retirement, where there are no fixed entrances or exits, and lots of sand into which it is easy to bury our heads."

Gail Sheehy

"I started using Grecian 2000 and now I look like a 2000-year-old Greek."

Roy Brown

"I actually think the whole concept of retirement is a bit stupid, so yes, I do want to do something else. There is this strange thing that just because chronologically on a Friday night you have reached a certain age... with all that experience, how can it be that on a Monday morning, you are useless?"

Stuart Rose

"The trouble with retirement is that you never get a day off."

Abe Lemons

"People talk to old people like they're children. 'Oh you're very old aren't you?' Yeah I'm old. I'm not stupid."

Craig Ferguson

"Old age is far more than white hair, wrinkles, the feeling that it is too late and the game finished, that the stage belongs to the rising generations. The true evil is not the weakening of the body, but the indifference of the soul."

André Maurois

"One starts to get young at the age of 60 and then it is too late."

Pablo Picasso

"People really get myopic as they get older. We're not a culture that encourages dreaming or distraction. We're not ever good at just being."

Karen Russell

"The head cannot take in more than the seat can endure."

Winston Churchill

"Old age is no place for sissies."
Bette Davis

"The years between 50 and 70 are the hardest. You are always being asked to do things and yet you are not decrepit enough to turn them down."
T. S. Eliot

"Those who think they have no time for bodily exercise will sooner or later have to find time for illness."
Edward Stanley

"You end up as you deserve. In old age you must put up with the face, the friends, the health and the children you have earned."

Judith Viorst

"With 60 staring me in the face, I have developed inflammation of the sentence structure and definite hardening of the paragraphs."

James Thurber

"A few of us who are around the 60 mark don't play that much these days, and if you are taking on a couple of guys in their forties it is very difficult."

John Newcombe

"You know you're 60 when it takes longer to rest than it did to get tired."

Anon

"Old age is an insult. It's like being smacked."

Lawrence Durrell

What They
Didn't
Tell You

"In youth we run into difficulties.
In old age difficulties run into us."

Beverly Sills

"As you get older, time speeds up,
but life slows down."

John C. Maxwell

"Bashfulness is an ornament to
youth, but a reproach to old age."

Aristotle

"Error is acceptable as long as we are young; but one must not drag it along into old age."

Johan Wolfgang von Goethe

"Have regular hours for work and play; make each day both useful and pleasant, and prove that you understand the worth of time by employing it well. Then youth will be delightful, old age will bring few regrets, and life will become a beautiful success."

Louisa May Alcott

"Everything slows down with age, except the time it takes cake and ice cream to reach your hips."

John Wagner

"He who is of a calm and happy nature will hardly feel the pressure of age, but to him who is of an opposite disposition, youth and age are equally a burden."

Plato

"I grabbed a pile of dust, and holding it up, foolishly asked for as many birthdays as the grains of dust. I forgot to ask that they be years of youth."

Ovid

"At 60, I know little more about wisdom than I did at 30, but I know a great deal more about folly."

Mason Cooley

"The excitement of learning separates youth from old age. As long as you're learning you're not old."

Rosalyn S. Yalow

"I will never be an old man. To me, old age is always 15 years older than I am."

Francis Bacon

"Is someone different at age 18 or 60? I believe one stays the same."

Hayao Miyazaki

"Experienced happiness refers to your feelings, to how happy you are as you live your life. In contrast, the satisfaction of the remembering self refers to your feelings when you think about your life."

Daniel Kahneman

"Grandchildren don't make a man feel old; it's the knowledge that he's married to a grandmother."

G. Norman Collie

"I've been accused of being old before my time more than once. It's true that I've always felt an affinity for, and been comfortable around, older people. I attribute this to a childhood spent around my grandparents – and even a great-grandparent or two. I wouldn't trade those experiences for anything."

Jon Meacham

"Looking 50 is great... if you're 60."

Joan Rivers

"In youth the days are short and the years are long. In old age the years are short and days long."

Pope Paul VI

"I'm 60 years of age. That's 16 Celsius."

George Carlin

·

"Maybe at 87 you slow down a drop, but between 44 and 64, there is no difference."

Jessica Hecht

"Youth is the time of getting,
middle age of improving and
old age of spending."

Anne Bradstreet

"Memory in youth is active and
easily impressible; in old age it
is comparatively callous to new
impressions, but still retains vividly
those of earlier years."

Charlotte Brontë

"Old age is a special problem for me because I've never been able to shed the mental image I have of myself – a lad of about 19."

E. B. White

"Preparation for old age should begin not later than one's teens. A life which is empty of purpose until 65 will not suddenly become filled on retirement."

Dwight L. Moody

"The old believe everything, the middle-aged suspect everything, the young know everything."

Oscar Wilde

"Twenty can't be expected to tolerate 60 in all things, and 60 gets bored stiff with 20's eternal love affairs."

Emily Carr

"You are only young once, but you can stay immature indefinitely."

Ogden Nash

"Old age is like everything else.
To make a success of it, you've
got to start young."

Theodore Roosevelt

"Maybe there is no actual place
called hell. Maybe hell is just
having to listen to our grandparents
breathe through their noses when
they're eating sandwiches."

Jim Carrey

Past It?

"A sexagenarian? At his age?
I think that's disgusting."

Gracie Allen

"You know you're getting old when
a four-letter word for something
pleasurable two people can do in
bed together is R-E-A-D."

Denis Norden

"All diseases run into one –
old age."

Ralph Waldo Emerson

"I'm getting to an age when I can only enjoy the last sport left. It's called hunting for your spectacles."

Edward Grey

"As long as possible, I would really like to complete one marathon per year. Though my time has been slowing down as I get older, it has become a very important part of my life."

Haruki Murakami

"My grandmother started walking five miles a day when she was 60. She's 97 now and we don't know where the hell she is."

Ellen DeGeneres

"Growing old isn't so bad, especially when you consider the alternative."

Anon

"Now that I'm 60 I wouldn't want to be a teenager again. But I wouldn't mind looking like one."

Melanie White

"Better to go than sit around being
a terrible old bore."

Auberon Waugh

"To me, if life boils down to one
thing, it's movement. To live
is to keep moving."

Jerry Seinfeld

"Not even old age knows how
to love death."

Sophocles

"Either God is alive, in which case he'll deal with us as he sees fit. Or he is dead, in which case he was never alive, it being unlikely that he died of old age."

John Ralston Saul

"I have a horror of leaving this world and not having anyone in the family know how to replace a toilet-roll holder."

Erma Bombeck

"If death meant just leaving the stage long enough to change costume and come back as a new character, would you slow down? Or speed up?"

Chuck Palahniuk

"To get back my youth I would do anything in the world, except take exercise, get up early or be respectable."

Oscar Wilde

"Imagine that if you could change one of the genes in an experiment, an ageing gene, maybe you could slow down ageing and extend lifespan."

Cynthia Kenyon

"It is old age, rather than death, that is to be contrasted with life. Old age is life's parody, whereas death transforms life into a destiny: in a way it preserves it by giving it the absolute dimension. Death does away with time."

Simone de Beauvoir

"Lord save us all from old age
and broken health and a hope tree
that has lost the faculty of putting
out blossoms."

Mark Twain

"Old age is always wakeful;
as if, the longer linked with life,
the less man has to do with aught
that looks like death."

Herman Melville

"I tend not to think about living to some grand old age. Then again, I don't think about dying, either."

Stella Young

"Remembering that you are going to die is the best way I know to avoid the trap of thinking you have something to lose. You are already naked. There is no reason not to follow your heart."

Steve Jobs

"The fear of old age is something that one feels when you're younger. Once you get to being old, you're already there, so you don't even think about it anymore."

Paolo Sorrentino

"The wiser mind mourns less for what age takes away than what it leaves behind."

William Wordsworth

"To keep the heart unwrinkled, to be hopeful, kindly, cheerful, reverent, that is to triumph over old age."

Amos Bronson Alcott

"I don't think kids have a problem with death. It's us older ones who are nearer to it that start being frightened."

Helena Bonham Carter

"Sex in the sixties is great, but it improves if you pull over to the side of the road."

Johnny Carson

"I keep fit. Every morning, I do a hundred laps of an Olympic-sized swimming pool – in a small motor launch."

Peter Cook

"To resist the frigidity of old age, one must combine the body, the mind and the heart. And to keep these in parallel vigor one must exercise, study and love."

Alan Bleasdale

"Try to keep your soul young and
quivering right up to old age."

George Sand

"You have to motivate yourself with
challenges. That's how you know
you're still alive."

Jerry Seinfeld

"Airplane travel is nature's way
of making you look like your
passport photograph."

Al Gore

"Death, like grandchildren, is one of the extraordinary new and exciting perks of old age. Over 60, it's time to get acquainted with it. No use dreading it or being frightened by it. People are always wringing their hands when their friends die, but frankly, what did they expect? That they'd live for ever?"

Virginia Ironside

"Men come of age at 60, women at 15."

James Stephens

"I've been married to my wife for 20 years. The Black Death lasted only three years."

Roy Brown

"The fear of death follows from the fear of life. A man who lives fully is prepared to die at any time."

Mark Twain

"Each year it grows harder to make ends meet – the ends I refer to are hands and feet."

Richard Armour

"Anyone who stops learning is old, whether at 20 or 80. Anyone who keeps learning stays young. The greatest thing in life is to keep your mind young."

Henry Ford

"I know it sounds weird, but my definition of 'sexy' has changed as I've gotten older. And being smart and informed makes me feel sexier than any outfit."

Sarah Shahi

"I guess I don't really believe in retirement. I believe in shorter days and maybe in weekends!"

Alice Walters

"Now that I'm over 60 I'm veering toward respectability."

Shelley Winters

"Retiring – within that word is 'tiring' and I'm not tired. I don't believe in retirement, really."

Theodore Bikel

"I'm getting old. When I squeeze into a tight parking space, I'm sexually satisfied for the day."

Rodney Dangerfield

"I'm hoping they slow down a little bit with technology, because I'm just trying to keep up."

Kate Upton

"The first thing I do when I wake up in the morning is breathe on a mirror and hop it fogs."

Earl Wynn

Celebrities
in Their
Sixties

"I'm kind of comfortable with getting older, because it's better than the other option, which is being dead. So I'll take getting older."

George Clooney

"I always say there's no point moaning about getting older, when there's nothing you can do about it. But still, I do find it quite funny. I look at that number, 60, and I think, really? Me?"

Twiggy

"With my sunglasses on, I'm Jack Nicholson. Without them, I'm fat and 60."

Jack Nicholson

"As you get older naked stuff gets easier. It's more to do with the role than what men in the audience think. There's a liberation about it."

Helen Mirren

"I'm comfortable being old... being black... being Jewish."

Billy Crystal

"I'm very f***ing grateful to be alive. I have so many friends who are sick or gone and I'm here. Are you kidding? No complaints!"

Meryl Streep

"Here is my biggest takeaway after 60 years on the planet: there is great value in being fearless. For too much of my life, I was too afraid, too frightened by it all. That fear is one of my biggest regrets."

Diane Keaton

"Being old is such a treat!"

Shirley MacLaine

"Do you really expect me to say gravity hasn't taken its toll? No. But as I'm earning these lines, I'm making an aesthetic choice."

Susan Sarandon

"Even if I don't want to slow down, I'm slowing down."

Eli Wallach

"Getting old is a fascinating thing.
The older you get, the older you
want to get."

Keith Richards

"I am really looking forward, as
I get older and older, to being less
and less nice."

Annette Bening

"I am aware of the words 'national
treasure' being attached to me
occasionally. It just makes me feel old."

Paul Weller

"As you get older, your metabolism slows down. You've got to admit it. It's nothing to be ashamed of if you have lived your life to the full."

Rod Stewart

"Don't retouch my wrinkles in the photograph. I would not want it to be thought that I had lived for all these years without having anything to show for it."

The Queen Mother

"I do know that [at] 60, I should be attempting to achieve different personal goals than those which had priority at age 20."

Warren Buffet

"You can live to be a hundred if you give up all the things that make you want to live to be a hundred."

Woody Allen

"I quite like being old."

Peter O'Toole

"I don't even think about a retirement program because I'm working for the Lord, for the Almighty. And even though the Lord's pay isn't very high, his retirement program is, you might say, out of this world."

George Foreman

"I feel the older I get, the more I'm learning to handle life. Being on this quest for a long time, it's all about finding yourself."

Ringo Starr

"Getting old is better than being young. You can do what you want to do."

Karl Pilkington

"I love being an advocate for women as we get older, so that we can feel comfortable with ourselves. It's all about being healthy for me now."

Andie MacDowell

"Growing older is not upsetting; being perceived as old is."

Kenny Rogers

"I think retirement's for old people.
I'm still in the business, thank you.
I have a young child of nine years
old and I want to live as long as
I can to see him grow up. I'm
enjoying my life and I want to stick
around for as long as I can."

Harrison Ford

"I'm not fiddling about with
myself... We're in this awful youth-
driven thing now where everybody
needs to look 30 at 60."

Emma Thompson

"I'd like to make time slow down."

Ryan Seacrest

"Sometimes I think it would be
easier to avoid old age, to die
young, but then you'd never
complete your life, would you?
You'd never wholly know you."

Marilyn Monroe

"I'm always announcing my
retirement. I'm still not retired."

Dick Van Dyke

"Making a Christmas album is looked upon by some people as the thing you do when you are heading towards retirement."

Annie Lennox

"Living is like tearing through a museum. Not until later do you really start absorbing what you saw, thinking about it, looking it up in a book, and remembering – because you can't take it in all at once."

Audrey Hepburn

"I feel alive, fit and active. I have no plans for retirement. My only concession to getting a little older is that I like to have a cat-nap in the afternoon. After that, I can push on through anything."

Olivia Newton-John

"I was afraid of being a failure, of not having the best time or of being chicken. But every year I get older I think, 'What was I fearing last year?' You forget. And then you move on."

Sandra Bullock

"Sixty felt like a big landmark. Not in a dreadful sense, but none of the other birthdays have bothered me. It's got labels on it – OAP, retirement – and I just wanted to take stock. I wanted to be in my greenhouse at home and at least give myself the opportunity of not working."

Julie Walters

"When I turned 60 it didn't bother me at all."

Yoko Ono

"The great thing about show business is that there's no mandatory retirement age."

Scott Bakula

"What could be more beautiful than a dear old lady growing wise with age? Every age can be enchanting, provided you live within it."

Brigitte Bardot

"So being present becomes more and more the exercise the older you get."

Paul Michael Glaser

"You could say that I'm resigned to the fact that this wonderful life that we get here is it. And having hit 60, it's a good time to get resigned to these things and not be too nervous or upset – and enjoy what great times one can have."

David Gilmour

"I love being an older comic now. It's like being an old soccer player or an old baseball player. You're in the Hall of Fame and it's nice, but you're no longer that person in the limelight on the spot doing that thing."

Eric Idle

"Your children are grown and your career has slowed down – all the stuff that took up so much attention is gone, and you're left with expansive time and space. You have to re-imagine who you are and what life is about."

Jessica Lange

"Youthfulness is about how you live not when you were born."

Karl Lagerfeld

"When I was a child, life felt so slow because all I wanted to do was get into show business. Each day seemed like a year, but when you get older, years pass like minutes. I wish there was a tape recorder where we could just slow our lives down."

Bruce Forsyth

"You get old, you slow down."

Ben Affleck

Words of Wisdom

"Remembering is painful, it's
difficult, but it can be inspiring
and it can give wisdom."

Paul Greengrass

"We've put more effort into
helping folks reach old age than
into helping them enjoy it."

Frank A. Clark

"If you're not getting happier as you
get older, then you're f***in' up."

Ani DiFranco

"Be kind to your kids. They'll choose your nursing home one day."

Anon

"My instruction to my parents is that I would rather they enjoy their retirement than leave me anything when they go. I am much happier watching them enjoying life."

Richard C. Armitage

"Old age begins when a person starts worrying about it."

Eduardo Albarracin Ramirez

"Wisdom doesn't necessarily come with age. Sometimes age just shows up all by itself."

Tom Wilson

"A tombstone is the only thing that can stand upright and lie on its face at the same time."

Mary Little

"I don't believe in ageing. I believe in forever altering one's aspect to the sun."

Virginia Woolf

"Most people don't know what's happening around them because they're just speeding through life. And before they know it, they're just old. So I just try to slow it down."

Tracy Morgan

"A man of 60 has spent 20 years in bed and over three years eating."

Arnold Bennett

"Old age and the passage of time teach all things."

Sophocles

"The older a man gets, the further he had to walk to school as a boy."

Josh Billings

"When I was younger, I could remember anything, whether it happened or not."

Mark Twain

"You know your children are growing up when they stop asking you where they come from and refuse to tell you where they are going."

P. J. O'Rourke

"If I'd known I was going to live
this long, I'd have taken better
care of myself."

Ubie Blake

"You are as young as your faith,
as old as your doubt; as young as
your self-confidence, as old as your
fear; as young as your hope,
as old as your despair."

Douglas MacArthur

"You know you are getting old when the candles cost more than the cake."

Bob Hope

"Count your age by friends, not years. Count your life by smiles, not tears."

John Lennon

"The teacher's life should have three periods: study until 25, investigation until 40, profession until 60, at which age I would have him retired on a double allowance."

William Osler

"Education is the best provision
for old age."

Aristotle

"Old age is just a record of one's
whole life."

Muhammad Ali

"The crucial task of old age is
balance: keeping just well enough,
just brave enough, just gay and
interested and starkly honest enough
to remain a sentient human being."

Florida Scott-Maxwell

"Never give up. The same manuscript may appeal to one agent and not to another. It's a matter of taste and it's all about the writing. What if I had given up at 15? Or 40? Or even 60?"

Kathryn Stockett

"We didn't have metaphors in our day. We didn't beat about the bush."

Fred Trueman

"Some people reach the age of 60 before others."

Lord Hood

"You know you're getting old when you get that one candle on the cake. It's like, 'See if you can blow this out.'"

Jerry Seinfeld

"Adulthood is the ever-shrinking period between childhood and old age. It is the apparent aim of modern industrial societies to reduce this period to a minimum."

Thomas Szasz

"Before you decide to retire, stay home for a week and watch the daytime TV shows."

Bill Copeland

"Lending money to your children is like lending money to a Third World country – you never get the interest back, let alone the principal."

J. L. Long

"Old age isn't so bad when you consider the alternative."

Maurice Chevalier

"The older I grow the more
I distrust the familiar doctrine
that age brings wisdom."

Henry L. Mencken

"And in the end, it's not the years in
your life that count. It's the life in
your years."

Abraham Lincoln

"Cherish all your happy moments;
they make a fine cushion for old age."

Booth Tarkington

"Old age is the most unexpected of all things that can happen to a man."

Leon Trotsky

"The key to immortality is first living a life worth remembering."

Bruce Lee

"There was no respect for youth when I was young, and now that I am old, there is no respect for age – I missed it coming and going."

J. B. Priestley

"The answer to old age is to keep one's mind busy and to go on with one's life as if it were interminable. I always admired Chekhov for building a new house when he was dying of tuberculosis."

Leon Edel

"Those who love deeply never grow old; they may die of old age, but they die young."

Dorothy Canfield Fisher

"You don't stop laughing because
you grow older. You grow older
because you stop laughing."

Maurice Chevalier

"The value of old age depends
upon the person who reaches it.
To some men of early performance
it is useless. To others, who are late
to develop, it just enables them to
finish the job."

Thomas Hardy

"Advice in old age is foolish; for what can be more absurd than to increase our provisions for the road the nearer we approach to our journey's end."

Cicero

"Age appears to be best in four things: old wood best to burn, old wine to drink, old friends to trust and old authors to read."

Francis Bacon

"Memory has always been fundamental for me. In fact, remembering what I had forgotten is the way most of the poems get started."

Seamus Heaney

"A comfortable old age is the reward of a well-spent youth. Instead of its bringing sad and melancholy prospects of decay, it would give us hopes of eternal youth in a better world."

Maurice Chevalier

"Youth is a blunder, manhood a struggle, old age a regret."

Benjamin Disraeli

"Old age adds to the respect due to virtue, but it takes nothing from the contempt inspired by vice; it whitens only the hair."

Ira Gershwin

"A man does not die of love or his liver or even of old age; he dies of being a man."

Miguel de Unamuno

"Old age is the verdict of life."

Amelia Barr

"Retirement may be looked upon
either as a prolonged holiday or
as a rejection, a being thrown
onto the scrap-heap."

Simone de Beauvoir

"Well-being changes as we move
through life, which is why a child's
version of it cannot be the same as
an old person's."

Deepak Chopra

"The older we grow the more
we realise that no one who is as
young as us is old."

Anon

"The first half of our lives is
ruined by our parents and the
second half by our children."

Clarence Darrow

"A legend is a lie that has attained
the dignity of old age."

H. L Mencken

Growing Old Gracefully?

"Old age is an excellent time for outrage. My goal is to say or do at least one outrageous thing every week."

Louis Kronenberger

"My doctor tells me I should start slowing it down – but there are more old drunks than there are old doctors, so let's all have another round."

Willie Nelson

"By the time you're 60, your address book... gets to be huge, and your writing tinier and tinier. Some names, sadly, have to go. I mean, are you ever really going to contact that delightful gay couple you had such fun with on a trip to Mongolia in 1978 again?"

Virginia Ironside

"Wrinkles should merely indicate where smiles have been."

Mark Twain

"I don't like the concept that
I am now, at 60, ageing. I've been
'ageing' since birth and not usually
in a graceful manner. Hang on to
what makes you different, special
and interesting."

Dan Antion

"How foolish to think that one can
ever slam the door in the face of
age. Much wiser to be polite and
gracious, and ask him to
lunch in advance."

Noel Coward

"The harvest of old age is the recollection and abundance of blessing previously secured."

Cicero

"Whether you are 16 or over 60, remember, understatement is the rule of a fine makeup artist."

Helen Rubinstein

"Alan Clark is not 65 going on 16. He is 65 going on 12."

Jane Clark

"Each child brings so much joy and hope into the world, and that is reason enough for being here. As you grow older, you will contribute something else to this world, and only you can discover what that is."

Sharon Creech

"My parents didn't want to move to Florida, but they turned 60 and that's the law."

Jerry Seinfeld

"When a noble life has prepared
for old age, it is not decline that it
reveals, but the first days
of immortality."

Madame de Stael

"I definitely am embracing ageing.
When you shoot your face with
Botox and stuff, you rob yourself
of your ability to have youthful
expressions, and that's why
sometimes people look a lot older."

Sheryl Crow

"I have reached an age when, if
someone tells me to wear socks,
I don't have to."

Albert Einstein

"My socks DO match. They have
the same thickness."

Steve Wright

"The longer I live the more
beautiful life becomes."

Frank Lloyd Wright

"The human brain can operate only as fast as the slowest brain cells. Excessive intake of alcohol kills brain cells, but naturally it attacks the slowest and weakest brain cells first. In this way, regular consumption of alcohol eliminates the weaker brain cells, making the brain a faster and more efficient machine."

W. C. Fields

"Growing old is mandatory; growing up is optional."

Chili Davis

"This whole getting older and being responsible thing is getting in the way of my fun."

Anon

"Ageing gracefully is one thing, but trying to slow it down is another."

Courteney Cox

"Please don't retouch my wrinkles. It took me so many birthdays to earn them."

Anna Magnani

"As we roll head-on into our sixties,
I ask myself, what's it going to be?
Are we to tiptoe quietly offstage?
I think not. Perhaps we want to stir
the stew some more, dare to live
large, to take changes. Maybe we
want to keep on trying to change
the world for the better. Or make a
scene. We do have practice in that."

Linda Ellerbee

"Retirement is not in my
vocabulary. They aren't going
to get rid of me that way."

Betty White

"When you are old and grey
and full of sleep,
And nodding by the fire,
take down this book,
And slowly read, and dream
of the soft look
Your eyes had once, and
of their shadows deep."

W. B. Yeats

"I enjoyed retirement the right
way... linguine con vongole, red
wine and plenty of truffle cheese."

Craig Kilborn

"I never understood the idea that
you're supposed to mellow as you get
older. Slowing down isn't something
I relate to at all. The goal is to
continue in good and bad, all of it."

Diane Keaton

"If we are strong, and have faith
in life and its richness of surprises,
and hold the rudder steadily in our
hands, I am sure we will sail into
quiet and pleasant waters for
our old age."

Freya Stark

"The secret of genius is to carry
the spirit of the child into old age,
which means never losing
your enthusiasm."

Aldous Huxley

"Abolish inheritance tax – no
taxation without respiration."

Bob Schaffer

"I prefer older men to younger men.
Older men can't run away so fast."

Jo Brand

"Ageing is not one process. It's many different things going on that cause us to age. I have a programme that at least slows down each of these different processes."

Ray Kurzweil

"Perhaps being old is having lighted rooms inside your head, and people in them, acting. People you know, yet can't quite name."

François de la Rochefoucauld

"Hitting 60 wasn't great, but
I think I was lucky in not being that
beautiful; it can be really cruel on
people who have been stunning."

Jane Birkin

"If retirement means laying on a
beach and rubbing coco butter on
your stomach, about 48 hours of
that will be enough for most people.
You'll want something new."

Timothy Ferriss

"In my youth I stressed freedom,
and in my old age I stress order.
I have made the great discovery
that liberty is a product of order."

Will Durant

"The secret of long life is double
careers. One to about age 60, then
another for the next 30 years."

David Ogilvy

"What, start at this!
When 60 years have spread
Their grey experience o'er
thy hoary head?
Is this the all observing age
could gain?
Or hast thou known the
world so long in vain?"

John Dryden

"I was brought up to respect my
elders, so now I don't have to
respect anybody."

George Burns

"Does there, I wonder, exist a being who has read all, or approximately all, that the person of average culture is supposed to have read, and that not to have read is a social sin? If such a being does exist, surely he is an old, a very old man."

Arnold Bennett

"A man is only as old as the woman he feels."

Groucho Marx

"One keeps forgetting old age up to
the very brink of the grave."

Sidonie-Gabrielle Colette

"Why should I fill in a census form?
I spent ages filling it in last time and
I didn't win a thing."

Giles Coren

"Don't simply retire from something;
have something to retire to."

Harry Emerson Fosdick

"Wisdom and penetration are the fruit of experience, not the lessons of retirement and leisure. Great necessities call out great virtues."

Abigail Adams

"Looking at 70 from 49, I don't see it slowing me down. Maybe I'll need a nap during the day! I'm thinking when I'm 85 I'll settle down a bit. But I'm going to fight, kicking and screaming, every step of the way."

Kyle MacLachlan

"Just 'cause there's snow on the roof doesn't mean there's not a fire inside."

Bonnie Hunt

"Many believe – and I believe – that I have been designated for this work by God. In spite of my old age, I do not want to give it up; I work out of love for God and I put all my hope in Him."

Michelangelo

"We must welcome the future,
remembering that soon it will be the
past; and we must respect the past,
remembering that it was once all
that was humanly possible."

George Santayana

"Old age, calm, expanded, broad
with the haughty breadth of the
universe, old age flowing free with the
delicious near-by freedom of death."

Edith Wharton

Celebrating
Your Sixties

"Wow! It took me 60 years to
look this good!"

Anon

"Be eccentric now. Don't wait for
old age to wear purple."

Regina Brett

"Age is strictly a case of mind over
matter. If you don't mind,
it doesn't matter."

Jack Benny

"Don't celebrate how old you are,
celebrate the years you survived."

Touaxia Vang

"It's not how old you are,
but how you are old."

Marie Dressler

"Don't think how old you are. Think
only of what you can accomplish.
Go! Do! This alone is living."

Peggy Mann

"On my 60th birthday my wife
gave me a superb birthday present.
She let me win an argument."

Anon

"With mirth and laughter let old
wrinkles come."

William Shakespeare, The Merchant of Venice

"Though it sounds absurd,
it is true to say I felt younger
at 60 than I felt at 20."

Ellen Glasgow

"How can they say my life is not a success? Have I not for more than 60 years got enough to eat and escaped being eaten?"

Logan Pearsall Smith

"Living each day as if it were your last doesn't mean your last day of retirement on a remote island. It means to live fully, authentically and spontaneously with nothing being held back."

Jack Canfield

"At 20 a man is a peacock,
at 30 a lion, at 40 a camel,
at 50 a serpent, at 60 a dog,
at 70 an ape, and at 80 nothing."

Baltasar Gracián

"People who 'hate getting old' are
idiots. Every year is a privilege.
Let me tell you, callow miserabilists:
getting to 60 feels like a triumph.
I have no idea how I made it this
far, but I am very grateful."

Ian Martin

"Your sixties can be one of the best – perhaps even the best – times of your life. You truly can savor your sixties."

Bonnie McFarland

"I found out retirement means playing golf – or I don't know what the hell it means. But to me, retirement means doing what you have fun doing."

Dick Van Dyke

"I wanted to teach myself some life
lessons at the age of 60 and one of
them was that you don't give up."

Diana Nyad

"Let us never know what old age
is. Let us know the happiness time
brings, not count the years."

Ausonius

"You're never too old
to stop learning."

Ian Botham

"I wanted to show I had balls at age 60. Just because society says I'm old, doesn't mean that I am. I'm pursuing happiness, even if it makes the people around me unhappy."

Sylvester Stallone

"I'm gonna enjoy being old. I think I'll be awesome at it."

Craig Ferguson

"You're a certified classic at 60!"

Dane Peddigrew

"I've joined a Keep Fat Club.
Every Wednesday morning we meet
and eat as many cakes as we can
manage."

Jo Brand

"Let us respect grey hairs,
especially our own."

J. P. Sears

"You're not getting older...
just more distinguished!"

Anon

"Old age is not a disease —
it is strength and survivorship,
triumph over all kinds of
vicissitudes and disappointments,
trials and illnesses."

Maggie Kuhn

"There is a fountain of youth:
it is your mind, your talents, the
creativity you bring to your life and
the lives of the people you love.
When you learn to tap this source,
you will have truly defeated age."

Sophia Loren

"I was born old and get younger
every day. At present I am
60 years young."

Herbert Beerbohm Tree

"Old age is not a matter for sorrow.
It is matter for thanks if we have left
our work done behind us."

Thomas Carlyle

"People who refuse to rest
honorably on their laurels when
they reach retirement age seem
very admirable to me."

Helen Hayes

"I got what no millionaire's got.
I got no money."

Gerald F. Lieberman

"If I had to live again,
I would do exactly the same thing.
Of course I have regrets, but if you
are 60 years old and you have no
regrets then you haven't lived."

Christy Moore

"It doesn't matter if you're
20, 40, 60, 80 or 100.
Embrace your sexy-ass self
and express it!"

Steve Maraboli